I0402551

How to Patent an Idea or Invention

A Step by Step Guide to Registering a Patent

By Meir Liraz

(Including 10 Special Bonuses)

Published by Liraz Publishing

www.BizMove.com

ISBN: 9781695865891

Table of Contents

MEIR LIRAZ

1. What is a Patent?

Because of the tremendous development and complexity of technology, products, and processes, manufacturers should be familiar with patent protection and procedures. It is important to understand patent rights and the relationships among a business, an inventor, and the Patent and Trademark Office to assure protection of your product and to avoid or win infringement suits. This guide gives some basic facts about patents to help clarify your rights in this important legal area.

To understand the details of patent procedure you should at the start know what a patent is and distinguish among patents, trademarks, and copyrights.

A patent is an exclusive property right to an invention. It gives an inventor the right to exclude others from making, using or selling an invention for a period of seventeen years in the United States, its territories, and possessions. A patent cannot be renewed except by act of Congress. Design patents for ornamental devices are granted for 3.5, 7 or 14 years - as th Because of the tremendous development and complexity of technology, products, and processes, manufacturers should be familiar with patent protection and procedures. It is important to understand patent rights and the relationships among a business, an inventor, and the Patent and Trademark Office to assure protection of your product and to avoid or win infringement suits. This guide gives some basic facts about patents to help clarify your rights in this important legal area.

To understand the details of patent procedure you should at the start know what a patent is and distinguish among patents, trademarks, and copyrights.

A patent is an exclusive property right to an invention. It gives an inventor the right to exclude others from making, using or selling an invention for a period of seventeen years in the United States, its territories, and possessions. A patent cannot be renewed except by act of Congress. Design patents for ornamental devices are granted for 3.5, 7 or 14 years - as the applicant elects.

Trademarks are also registered by the Commissioner of Patents and Trademarks on application by individuals or companies who distinguish, by name or symbol, a product used in commerce subject to regulation by Congress. They can be registered for a period of twenty years.

Copyrights, administered by the Copyright Office (Library of Congress, Washington, DC), protect authors, composers, and artists from the "pirating" of their literary and artistic work.

2. First Steps

When you get an idea for a product or process that you think is mechanically sound and likely to be profitable, write down your idea. Consider specifically what about your new device is original or patentable and superior to similar devices already on the market (and patented). Your idea should be written in a way that provides legal evidence of its origin because your claim could be challenged later. Next you need help to determine your device's novelty and to make a proper application for a patent.

Professional Assistance. Professional assistance is recommended strongly because patent procedures are quite detailed. Also, you may not know how to make use of all the technical advantages available. For instance, you may not claim broad enough protection for your device. As a rule therefore, it is best to have your application filed by a patent lawyer or agent.

Only attorneys and agents who are registered with the Patent Office may prosecute an application. It will not, however recommend any particular attorney or agent, nor will it assume responsibility for your selection.

Establishing Novelty. This is one of the most crucial and difficult determinations to make, involving two things: 1) analyzing the device according to specified standards and 2) seeing whether or not anyone else has patented it first. The only sure way of accomplishing this is to make a search of Patent Office files.

Analyzing your device. This should be done according to the following standards of what is patentable:

(1) Any new, useful, and unobvious process (primarily industrial or technical); machine; manufacture or composition of matter (generally chemical compounds, formulas, and the like); or any new, useful, and unobvious improvement thereof;

(2) Any new and unobvious original and ornamental design for an article of manufacture, such as a new auto body design, (Note that a design patent may not always turn out to be valuable because a commercially similar design can easily be made without infringing the patent);

(3) Any distinct and new variety of plant, other than tubes-propagated, which is asexually reproduced.

Another way of analyzing your product is to consider it in relation to what is not patentable, as follows:

(1) An idea (as opposed to a mechanical device);

(2) A method of doing business (such as the assembly line system; however, any structural or mechanical innovations employed might constitute patentable subject matter;

(3) Printed matter (covered by copyright law);

(4) An inoperable device;

(5) An improvement in a device which is obvious or the result of mere mechanical skill (a new assembly of old parts or an adaptation of an old principle - aluminum window frames instead of the conventional wood).

Applications for patents on machines or processes for producing fissionable material can be filed with the Patent and Trademark Office. In most instances, however, such applications might be withheld if the subject matter affects national security and for that reason should not be made public.

The invention should also be tested for novelty by the following criteria:

(1) Whether or not known or used by others in this country before the invention by the applicant;

(2) Whether or not patented or described in a printed publication in this or a foreign country before the invention by the applicant;

(3) Whether or not described in a printed publication more than one year prior to the date of application for patent in the United States.

(4) Whether or not in public use or on sale in the country more than one year prior to the date of application for patent in the United States.

These points are important. For example, if you describe a new device in a printed publication or use it publicly or place it on sale, you must apply for a patent before one year has gone by; otherwise you lose any right to a patent.

Although marking your product "patent pending" after you have applied has no legal protective effect, it often tends to ward off potential infringers.

Search of existing patents and technical literature. It is not necessary for you or your attorney to travel personally to Arlington, VA to make a search of Patent and Trademark Office files. Arrangements can be made with associates in Arlington, VA to have this done.

Only the files of patents granted are open to the public. Pending applications are kept in strictest secrecy and no access is given to them except on written authority of the applicants or their duly authorized representatives. Existing patents may be consulted in the Search Room of the Patent and Trademark Office where records of over 4,000,000 patents issued since 1836 are maintained. In addition, over 9,000,000 copies of foreign patents may also be seen in the Patent Library. That library contains a quantity of scientific books and periodicals which may carry a description of your idea and thus affect its patentability.

A search of patents, besides indicating whether or not your device is patentable, may also prove informative. It may disclose patents superior to your device but not already in production which might profitably be manufactured and sold by your company. A valuable business association may result.

3. Points of Caution

While the advantages of obtaining a patent are fairly obvious, it must be recognized that a number of pitfalls and obstacles lurk in the path of every applicant. For example, a patent by no means guarantees immunity from lawsuits, but rather sometimes seems to attract challenges to its legality. As one patent lawyer has said. "A patent is merely a fighting interest in a lawsuit."

Interference. One of these snags is interference (occurring in about only one percent of the cases) when two or more applicants have applications pending for substantially the same invention. Because a patent should be granted to only one applicant, the parties in such a case must give proof of the date the invention was made. Ordinarily, the applicant who proves that he or she was the first to conceive the invention and produce a working device will be held to be the prior inventor. If no other evidence is submitted, the date of filing the applications is used to settle the controversy. Priority questions are determined on evidence submitted to a board of examiners.

Infringement. Unauthorized manufacture, use, or

sale of subject matter embraced by the claims of a patent constitutes infringement. The patent owner may file suit in for damages and/or an injunction prohibiting the continued use or manufacture of the patented article. If an item is not marked "patented," the holder of the patent may sue for damages on account of infringement but no damages can be received covering the period before the infringer is so notified.

Moreover, no recovery of damages is possible for any infringement occurring more than six years before the filing of the complaint. There is no established method of learning of any infringement. A clipping service and a sharp eye for reference in trade literature may be helpful, but the responsibility lies entirely with the patentee (patent holder).

Foreign Patents. If you wish to market your patented product in a foreign country, you should apply for patent protection in the particular country to prevent infringement.

Selling Part Interest. Once you get a patent, consider how to make the best use of it. You have several choices of action. If you have the facilities and money, you can manufacture and sell the article. Alternatively, you can sell all or part of the patent or you can license or assign it to someone else.

Probably the trickiest operation of all is selling part interest in a patent. Remember that joint ownership holds many pitfalls unless restricted by a contract. A joint owner, no matter how small his or her interest, may use the patent as the original owner. He may make use of or sell the item for his own profit, without regard to any other owner, and he may also sell his interest in it to someone else. A new part owner is responsible for making sure that any such transfer is recorded within three months at the Patent and Trademark Office.

This is what could happen. An inventor offers to sell this patent for $500,000, but the prospective buyer, claiming this is too expensive, proposes to buy part interest of say $50,000 or ten percent interest in it. If the sale were concluded, the new part owner-unless specifically restrained from doing so by contract- could go ahead and manufacture and sell the item as if he owned it 100 percent, without accounting to the other part owner (who is the original investor and patent holder).

Assignments and Licenses. A patent is personal property and can be sold or even mortgaged. You can sell or transfer a patent or patent application. Such a transfer of interest is an assignment; and the assignee then has the rights to the patent that the original patentee had. A whole or part interest can be assigned.

Like an assignment, a grant conveys an interest in a patent but only for a specified area of the United States.

A mortgage of patent property gives ownership to the lender for the duration of the loan.

You can license your patent which means someone pays you for the right to your patent according to the conditions of the license.

All assignments, grants, licensees, or conveyances of any patent or application for a patent should be notarized and must be recorded with the Patent and Trademark Office within three months of the transfer of rights. If not, it is void against a subsequent buyer unless it is recorded prior to the subsequent purchase.

All references and documents relating to a patent or

a patent application should be identified by the number, date, inventor's name and the title of the invention. Adequate identification will lessen the difficulties of determining ownership rights and what patents and applications are in issue.

Other Problems You Confront as an Inventor. Even though your invention passes the expert, impartial judgment of a patent examiner as to novelty and workability, it still must be commercially acceptable if you are to make money from it. In this respect you should expect no help for the Patent and Trademark Office, as it can offer no advice on this point.

Also, you should realize that, in modern technology, the vast majority of patents granted are merely improvements or refinements on a basic invention. The claims allowed on an improvement patent are narrow, as compared with those of a basic invention. Because the claims allowed on an improvement patent are narrow as compared with those of a basic patent, the inventor therefore runs a proportionately greater risk of infringement if a basic patent is in force.

Here is an example: Inventor George Westinghouse

patented an entirely new device - the air brake. For this he was granted broad protection by the Patent and Trademark Office. Suppose that later, inventor "B" devised a structural improvement, such as a new type of valve for the compressed air. Inventor "B" would have received relatively narrow protection on the valve and could not have been able to manufacture the complete air brake without infringing Westinghouse's patent. Nor could anyone else to whom "B" licensed the patent make the whole brake.

Also, be aware that United States patent laws make no discrimination with respect to the citizenship of an inventor. Regardless of citizenship, any inventor may apply for a patent on the same basis as an American citizen.

Finally, purchasing is an important aspect of all business and touches upon patents. Purchase orders can have clauses dealing with patent infringement. Practice, type of goods, and many factors affect the clause; but such a clause could be as follows:

Seller shall indemnify and save harmless the buyer and/or its vendees from and against all cost, expenses, and damages arising out of any infringement or claim of infringement of any patent or patents in the use of articles or equipment furnished hereunder.

4. Application for a Patent

If you find, after preliminary search, that your invention appears to be patentable, the next step is the preparation of a patent application covering your invention. File it with the Commissioner of Patents and Trademarks, Washington, DC 20231. All subsequent correspondence should also be addressed to the Commissioner.

The Patent Application. With few exceptions the patent application must be filed in the name of the inventor. Even the application for a patent on an invention by a company's researcher must be filed in the inventor's name. If there is more than one inventor, a joint application is made. The patent application can be assigned, however, to an individual or a corporation, and then the patent will be granted to the assignee, although filed in the inventor's name.

Often employment agreements require an employee to assign to the employer any invention relating to the employer's business. Even without such an agreement, the employer may have a "shop right" to use (free) an invention developed on the job by an employee.

Application for a patent is made to the Commissioner of Patents and Trademarks and includes:

(1) A written document that comprises a petition, a specification (descriptions and claims), and an oath;

(2) A drawing in those cases in which a drawing is possible; and

(3) A filing fee.

The exacting requirements of the Patent and Trademarks Office for a patent application are described in Title 37, Code of Federal Regulation, which may be purchased from the Superintendent of Documents; Government Printing Office, Washington, DC 20402.

The construction of the invention, its operation, and its advantages should be accurately described. From the "disclosure" of the application, any person skilled in the field of the invention should be able to understand the intended construction and use of the invention. Commercial advantages, which would be attractive to a prospective manufacturer, need not be discussed.

The claims at the end of the specification point out

the patentably new features of the invention. Drawings must be submitted according to rigid Patent and Trademark Office regulations.

The filing fee is normally paid by check, payable to the Commissioner of Patents and Trademarks or by a money order sent by registered mail. The Patent and Trademark Office assumes no responsibility for its safe arrival.

What Happens to Your Application in the Patent Office. When your application is received in the Patent and Trademark Office, it is given a preliminary examination to determine whether or not all requirements are met. If The application is in order, you will be notified of that fact and your application assigned a serial number and filing date. These govern its position on the docket. If there is some very minor deficiency, such as some irregularity in the drawings, the date and number will be assigned and the necessary revision requested later. If the application is incomplete, you will be notified and your application will be held up until you supply the required information to correct the deficiency.

After your application is filed, it is examined by an

examiner trained and experienced in the field of your invention. Frequently, the examiner finds existing patents showing inventions enough like yours that revision of the application claims will have to be make. Sometimes several revisions and arguments by your patent attorney (or agent) are necessary to overcome successive objections raised by the examiner. Each objection constitutes and action by the Patent and Trademark Office; and if no response is made to an action within a prescribed period, the application is considered abandoned. An abandoned application is dropped from further consideration. Because each application must ordinarily await its turn to be considered or reconsidered, it generally takes on the average of nineteen months to get a patent.

If the examiner finally refuses to grant a patent on the basis of the claims requested, the application may be appealed to the Board of Appeals of the Patent Office. A brief for this appeal must be filed within sixty days after the date of the appeal.

When all the examiner's objections are satisfied, a patent may be obtained by payment of a final fee. A brief description of each patent issued is published weekly in the Official Gazette of the U.S. Patent

Office. At the same time, specifications and drawings of current issuances are published separately, and copies are generally available to the public.

Making Applications Special. Only under limited conditions may a petition be filed requesting that an application be given special treatment; that is, taken up for examination before its normal turn is reached. These requirements are of particular importance to small business owners who are eager to obtain a patent before starting a manufacturing program. If you ask for special treatment for that reason, you must state under oath:

(1) That you have sufficient capital available and facilities to manufacture the invention in quantity. If you are acting as an individual, there must also be a corroborating affidavit from an officer of a bank, showing that you have obtained sufficient capital to manufacture the invention.

(2) That you will not manufacture unless it is certain that the patent will be granted.

(3) That you will obligate yourself or your company to produce the invention in quantity as soon as patent protection has been established. A

corporation must have this commitment agreed to in writing by its board of directors.

(4) That if the application is allowed, you will furnish a statement under oath within three months of such allowance, showing (a) how much money has been expended, (b) the number of devices manufactured, and (c) labor employed.

Your attorney must file an affidavit to show that he or she has made a careful and thorough search of the prior art and believes all the claims in the application are allowable. The attorney will also be expected to make sure that the last sworn statement described above is properly filed.

As distinguished from mechanical patents, there are also available patents to protect ornamental designs for articles of manufacture.

5. Plant Patents

Plant patents were introduced in 1930. A plant patent is granted to an inventor (or his heirs or assigns) who has invented (or discovered) and asexually reproduced a distinct and new variety of plant. Plant seedlings discovered, propagated asexually, and proved to have new characteristics distinct from other known plants are patentable. Tuber-propagated plants (such as potatoes and artichokes) or plants found in the uncultivated state are not patentable. Tuber-propagated plants are excluded because, among asexually reproduced plants, they are propagated by the same part of the plant that is sold as food.

The grant is the right to exclude others from asexually reproducing the plant, or selling, or using the plant so reproduced. Patented plants must have new characteristics which distinguish them from others, such as resistance to drought, cold, or heat. They must also not have been introduced to the public nor placed on sale more than one year before the filing of a patent application.e applicant elects.

Trademarks are also registered by the Commissioner of Patents and Trademarks on application by individuals or companies who distinguish, by name or symbol, a product used in commerce subject to regulation by Congress. They can be registered for a period of twenty years.

Copyrights, administered by the Copyright Office (Library of Congress, Washington, DC), protect authors, composers, and artists from the "pirating" of their literary and artistic work.

6. How to Make the Right Decisions

Everyone is a decision maker. We all rely on information, and techniques or tools, to help us in our daily lives. When we go out to eat, the restaurant menu is the tool that provides us with the information needed to decide what to purchase and how much to spend. Operating a business also requires making decisions using information and techniques - how much inventory to maintain, what price to sell it at, what credit arrangements to offer, how many people to hire.

Decision making in business is the systematic process of identifying and solving problems, of asking questions and finding answers. Decisions usually are made under conditions of uncertainty. The future is not known and sometimes even the past is suspect. This guide opens the door for business owners and managers to learn about the variety of techniques which can be used to improve decision making in a world of uncertainty, change, and uncontrollable circumstances.

A General Approach to Decision Making

Whether a scientist, an executive of a major corporation, or a small business owner, the general approach to systematically solving problems is the same. The following 7 step approach to better management decision making can be used to study nearly all problems faced by a business.

1. State the problem

A problem first must exist and be recognized. What is the problem and why is it a problem. What is ideal and how do current operations vary from that ideal. Identify why the symptoms (what is going wrong) and the causes (why is it going wrong). Try to define all terms, concepts, variables, and relationships. Quantify the problem to the extent possible. If the problem, not accurately and quickly filling customer orders, try to determine how many orders were incorrectly filled and how long it took to fill them.

2. Define the Objectives

What are the objectives of the study. Which objectives are the most critical. Objectives usually are stated by an action verb like to reduce, to increase, or to improve. Returning to the customer order problem, the major objectives would be: 1) to increase the percentage of orders filled correctly, and 2) to reduce the time it takes to process and order. A subobjective could include to simplify and streamline the order filling process.

3. Develop a Diagnostic Framework

Next establish a diagnostic framework, that is, decide what methods are going to be used, what kinds of information are needed, and how and where the information is to be found. Is there going to be a customer survey, a review of company documents, time and motion tests, or something else. What are the assumptions (facts assumed to be correct) of the study. What are the criteria used to judge the study. What time, budget, or other constraints are there. What kind of quantitative or other specific techniques are going to be used to analyze the data. (Some of which will be covered shortly). In other words, the diagnostic framework establishes the scope and methods of the entire study.

4. Collect and Analyze the Data

The next step is to collect the data (by following the methods established in Step 3. Raw data is then tabulated and organized to facilitate analysis. Tables, charts, graphs, indexes and matrices are some of the standard ways to organize raw data. Analysis is the

MEIR LIRAZ

critical prerequisite of sound business decision making. What does the data reveal. What facts, patterns, and trends can be seen in the data. Many of the quantitative techniques covered below can be used during the step to determine facts, patterns, and trends in data. Of course, computers are used extensively during this step.

5. Generate Alternative Solutions

After the analysis has been finished, some specific conclusions about the nature of the problem and its resolution should have been reached. The next step is to develop alternative solutions to the problem and rank them in order of their net benefits. But how are alternatives best generated. Again, there are several well established techniques such as the Nominal Group Method, the Delphi Method and Brainstorming, among others. In all these methods a group is involved, all of whom have reviewed the data and analysis. The approach is to have an informed group suggesting a variety of possible solutions.

6. Develop an Action Plan and Implement

Select the best solution to the problem but be certain to understand clearly why it is best, that is,

32

how it achieves the objectives established in Step 2 better than its alternatives. Then develop an effective method (Action Plan) to implement the solution. At this point an important organizational consideration arises - who is going to be responsible for seeing the implementation through and what authority does he have. The selected manager should be responsible for seeing that all tasks, deadlines, and reports are performed, met, and written. Details are important in this step: schedules, reports, tasks, and communication are the key elements of any action plan. There are several techniques available to decision makers implementing an action plan. The PERT method is a way of laying out an entire period such as an action plan. PERT will be covered shortly.

7. Evaluate, obtain Feedback and Monitor

After the Action Plan has been implemented to solve a problem, management must evaluate its effectiveness. Evaluation standards must be determined, feedback channels developed, and monitoring performed. This Step should be done after 3 to 5 weeks and again at 6 months. The goal is to answer the bottom line question. Has the problem been solved?

7. Improving Your Delegation Skills

Derived from Latin, delegate means "to send from." When delegating you are sending the work "from" you "to" someone else. Effective delegation Skills will not only give you more time to work on your important opportunities, but you will also help others on your team learn new skills.

Here are some tips that will help you improve your delegation skills - delegation of work.

- Delegation helps people grow underneath you in an organization and thus pushes you even higher in management. It provides you with more time, and you will be able to take on higher priority projects.

- Delegate whole pieces or entire job pieces rather than simply tasks and activities.

- Clearly define what outcome is needed, then let individuals use some creative thinking of their own as to how to get to that outcome.

- Clearly define limits of authority that go with the delegated job. Can the person hire other people to work with them? Are there spending constraints?

- Clear standards of performance will help the person know when he or she is doing exactly what is expected.

- When on the receiving end of delegation, work to make your boss' job easier and to get the boss promoted. This will enhance your promotability also.

- Assess routine activities in which you are involved. Can any of them be eliminated or delegated?

- Never underestimate a person's potential. Delegate slightly more than you think the person is capable of handling. Expect them to succeed, and you will be pleasantly surprised more frequently than not.

- Expect completed staff work from the individuals reporting to you. That is, they will come to you giving you alternatives and suggestions when a problem exists rather than just saying "Boss, what should we do?"

- Do not avoid delegating something because you cannot give someone the entire project. Let the person start with a bite size piece, then after learning and doing that, they can accept larger pieces and larger areas of responsibility.

- Agree on a monitoring or measurement procedure that will keep you informed as to progress on this project because you are ultimately still responsible for it and need to know that it is progressing as it should. In other words-If you can't measure it don't delegate it.

- Keep your mind open to new ideas and ways of doing things. There just might be a better way than the way something has previously been done.

- Delegation is not giving an assignment. You are asking the person to accept responsibility for a project. They have the right to say no.

- Encourage your people to ask for parts of your job.

- Never take back a delegated item because you can do it better or faster. Help the other person learn to do it better.

- Agree on the frequency of feedback meetings or reports between yourself and the person to whom you are delegating. Good communication will assure ongoing success.

- Delegation strengthens your position. It shows you are doing your job as a manager-getting results with others. This makes you more promotable.

- Delegation is taking a risk that the other person might make a mistake, but people learn from mistakes and will be able to do it right the next time. Think back to a time a project was delegated to you and you messed it up. You also learned a valuable lesson.

- Find out what the talents and interests of your people are and you will be able to delegate more intelligently and effectively.

- A person will be more excited about doing a project when they came up with the idea of how to do it, than if the boss tells them how to do it.

- Be sensitive to upward delegation by your staff. When they ask you for a decision on their project, ask them to think about some alternatives which you will then discuss with them. This way responsibility for action stays with the staff member.

- Don't do an activity that someone else would be willing to do for you if you would just ask them.

- "Push" responsibility down in a caring helpful way.

- Remember, you are not the only one that can accomplish an end result. Trust others to be capable of achieving it.

- Break large jobs into manageable pieces and delegate pieces to those who can do them more readily.

- Keep following up and following through until the entire project is done. Break large jobs into manageable pieces and delegate pieces to those who can do them more readily.

- Resist the urge to solve someone else's problem. They need to learn for themselves. Give them suggestions and perhaps limits but let them take their own action.

Appendix: Special Free Bonuses

You can access your free bonuses here:

https://www.bizmove.com/bizgifts.htm

Here's what you get:

#1 How to Be a Good Manager and Leader; 120 Tips to improve your Leadership Skills (Leadership Video Guide).

Learn how to improve your leadership skills and become a better manager and leader. Here's how to be the boss people want to give 200 percent for. In this video you'll discover 120 powerful tips and strategies to motivate and inspire your people to bring out the best in them.

#2 Small Business Management: Essential Ingredients for Success (eBook Guide)

Discover scores of business management tricks, secrets and shortcuts. This Ebook guide does far more than impart knowledge - it inspires action.

#3 How to Manage Yourself for Success; 90 Tips to Better Manage Yourself and Your Time (Self Management Video Guide)

You are responsible for everything that happens in your life. Learn to accept total responsibility for yourself. If you don't manage yourself, then you are letting others have control of your life. In this video you'll discover 90 powerful tips and strategies to better manage yourself for success.

#4 80 Best Inspirational Quotes for Success (Motivational Video Guide)

For this video we scanned thousands of motivational and inspirational quotes to bring you this collection of the best 80 motivational quotes for success in life.

#5 Top 10 Habits to Adopt From Highly Successful People (Self Growth Video Guide)

In this video you'll discover the top 10 habits of highly successful people that you can adopt and achieve success in your life.

#6 Personal Branding: How to Make a Killer First Impression (Self Promotion Video Guide)

This video deals with personal branding. While promoting your personal brand, you'll discover in this video the ten most effective things you can do to make the best first impression possible.

#7 How to Advance Your Career 10 Times Faster (Career Advancement Video Guide)

The most important thing to remember about your

career today is that you need to be responsible for your own future. In this video you'll discover 10 powerful strategies to advance your career faster.

#8 How to Get Success in Life; 10 Strategies to Attract the Life You Want (Self Actualization Video Guide)

To have more, we must be more of who we are. The secret is in the doing; none of it matters until we do something about it. In this video you'll discover 10 powerful strategies to attract the life you want.

#9 A Comprehensive Package of Business Tools

Here's a collection featuring dozens of business related templates, worksheets, forms, and plans; covering finance, starting a business, marketing, business planning, sales, and general management.

#10 People Management Skills: How to Deal with Difficult Employees (Managing People Video Guide)

Problem behavior on the part of employees can erupt for a variety of reasons. In this video you'll discover the top ten ideas for dealing with difficult employees.

* * * *

www.ingramcontent.com/pod-product-compliance
Lightning Source LLC
Chambersburg PA
CBHW070842220526
45466CB00002B/859